ANGELS

A journey of exploration for individuals, small groups or churches

Robert and Ro Willoughby

The Messengers Series: **ANGELS** by Robert and Ro Willoughby
Scripture Union, 207–209 Queensway, Bletchley, MK2 2EB, UK
e-mail: info@scriptureunion.org.uk
www.scriptureunion.org.uk

Scripture Union Australia: Locked Bag 2, Central Coast Business Centre, NSW 2252
www.su.org.au

ISBN 1 84427 223 0
EAN 978 184427 223 5

First published in Great Britain by Scripture Union 2006

British Library Cataloguing-in-Publication data: a catalogue record for this book is available from the British Library.

Cover design by David Lund Design, Milton Keynes

Internal illustrations by Helen Gale

Internal page design by Creative Pages: www.creativepages.co.uk

Printed and bound by Henry Ling Limited, Dorchester, UK

Scripture Union is an international Christian charity working with churches in more than 130 countries providing resources to bring the good news about Jesus Christ to children, young people and families – and to encourage them to develop spiritually through the Bible and prayer. As well as a network of volunteers, staff and associates who run holidays, church-based events and school Christian groups, Scripture Union produces a wide range of publications and supports those who use their resources through training programmes.

Contents

Real experiences

Drama scripts

Creative activities/photocopiable sheets

The artist's view

Book excerpts

Robert and Ro Willoughby

introduce

ANGELS

Angels are everywhere! That's what we've discovered while we've been writing this material. It has been extraordinary just how often we have caught each other's eye while out shopping or chatting to people and angels have been evident in the merchandise around us or in topics of conversations. But particularly in church, of course. We've nudged each other during the singing of a hymn which 'just happens' to mention angels or we've listened to a Bible reading in which, yet again, angels get a mention. They are frequently present in the Bible, if you care to look for them!

Sadly very few Protestant theologians or commentators give them much space. Maybe it's the remnants of anxiety about the rather exotic miracles and visions of angels which were very prominent in the late Middle Ages in Europe. Or perhaps theologians today are concerned not to give too much space to what might be mistaken for New Age spirituality. It seems a pity that so few thinkers have given them the attention they deserve.

Even more sadly, many Christians dismiss the whole idea of the existence of angels out of hand. Some rank them alongside goblins, fairies or elves – as fantasy or the product of a Tolkienesque imagination. Some people can't imagine why God would need to create them or make use of them. It doesn't help that angels are sometimes depicted in ways which are simply ridiculous. The truth is, Scripture gives us very little idea of what they might look like. Wings? White garments?

This book is written from a Christian perspective and is based on the Christian Scriptures. Certainly there is much interest in angels today across society; we are well aware that a lot of non-Christians – from other religious traditions or none – believe in angels. The testimony of scripture is consistent: angels do exist. Why should we assume that God's creation consists only of what we can see, feel, hear, touch – in a word, measure? Could not Almighty God, if he so wished, create a universe which is peopled by huge numbers of beings which we simply cannot apprehend with our limited senses? The Bible assumes that he could, and that he did.

Despite what we have said about the absence of attention from theologians, there are some exceptions. In the sixteenth century, the reformer John Calvin wrote 23 pages about angels in his *Institutes of the Christian Religion*. In the twentieth century Karl Barth thought that angels were such an important point of contact between this world and eternity that he devoted over 150 pages to them in his massive *Church Dogmatics*. At a much more popular level Billy Graham's book *Angels: God's Secret Agents* and Hope Price's *Angels: True Stories of How They Touch Our Lives* are more contemporary contributions. But such books used to be few and far between.

We could speculate why these non-attention-seeking heavenly beings who apparently make such a celestial choral clatter and are so central to the fulfilment of God's purposes on earth receive so little attention. But, after all, they are not really what the Bible is all about: angels are God's agents. They serve *him*. The snippets of information or insight that we gain from the Bible portray them as a bit mysterious, strange and sometimes a little frightening. However, because they frequently appear at key moments in God's dealings with humanity there is much to be gained by studying them. Karl Barth wrote, 'Where God is, there the angels of God are ... where there are no angels, there is no God.'

Interest in them *is* growing. We hope that this resource book – whether used in a church, small group, youth group or by you on your own – will awaken your enthusiasm for and expectation of angelic beings!

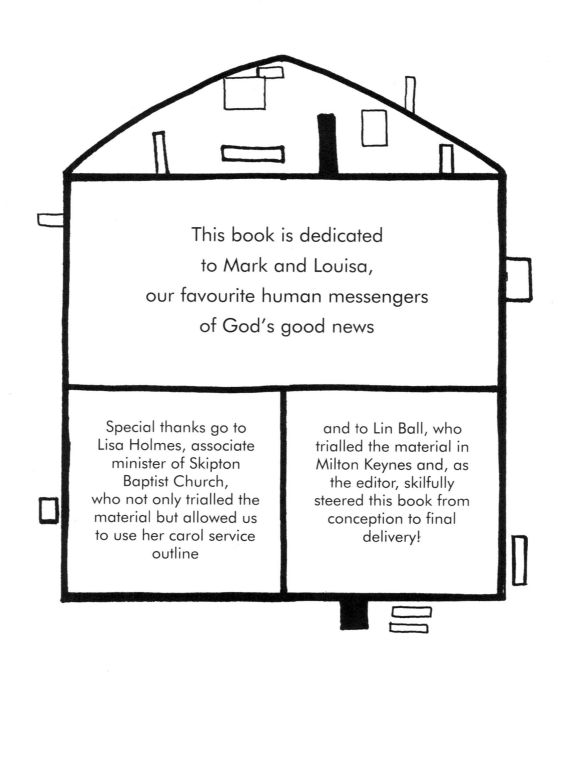

This book is dedicated
to Mark and Louisa,
our favourite human messengers
of God's good news

Special thanks go to
Lisa Holmes, associate
minister of Skipton
Baptist Church,
who not only trialled the
material but allowed us
to use her carol service
outline

and to Lin Ball, who
trialled the material in
Milton Keynes and, as
the editor, skilfully
steered this book from
conception to final
delivery!

When and how to use

ANGELS

Many Christians make brilliant jugglers – keeping all their responsibilities going like spinning plates. They manage their careers, cope with the demands of family life – *and* find time to nurture their relationship with God, contribute to the life of their Christian community and remain whole people! Finding additional time to explore the Bible, either with others or on their own, can be asking a lot.

So, recognising the complex stresses of contemporary life, the key feature of this material is flexibility. It can be used at any time of the year and in a variety of ways. It's a resource book for church or youth leaders to dip into. It can be used within the small group setting in homes – either to run a four-session course by selecting from the 'menu' of activities or to run a longer course by working more systematically through the material, using each of the four sections of the book for two or more sessions. It could be used as core material for a church family away-day or celebration day – particularly during the Christmas season; or – given the general interest in the subject of angels – for a series of evangelistic evening or weekend seminars. And there would be much to be gained by the individual wanting to study angels using this material, though obviously some of the discussion questions or more elaborate craft options would be less appropriate.

ANGELS in Advent

One of the best times to use ANGELS is during Advent. Yes, this time of year is even more fraught than usual! To all the usual spinning plates will be added the stresses of Christmas shopping, office parties, school concerts, family gatherings and so on. But there is so much to be gained by making spiritual preparation for this important time in the Christian calendar. The activities that are specifically seasonal are indicated by a holly sprig, so if you are using ANGELS at a different time of year you might want to skip or adapt those – although there is a strong case to be made for celebrating the Incarnation other than at Christmastime!

The churches and small groups who tried out this material used it during Advent and many people found that they could squeeze in four two-hour slots to meet in groups in late November and December and that, as a result, they felt much more spiritually ready for Christmas. The activities are designed to be fun as well as thought-provoking, so fit well into the more 'social' framework of life at this time of year; and we've tried to keep leader's preparation time to a minimum. One of the groups who trialled ANGELS were busy parents who dropped off their sons and daughters at a young people's group on a Sunday evening. They met as an alternative group for four weeks during Advent – their meeting lasting just as long as the youth session did! Another group put a special emphasis on prayer for their church's Christmas week services – something which particularly gladdened the heart of their minister.

To make this material as useful as possible, we also added in some sermon outlines, an outline for an all-age event for use at any time of the year, and a plan for a carol service focused on angels.

Tried and tested

We'd like to thank everyone involved in testing ANGELS. The material was used in three churches:

Croxley Green Baptist Church (near Watford), Skipton Baptist Church and Spurgeon Baptist Church (Milton Keynes). These were coincidentally all Baptist churches – but we hope that the material has a wide appeal across different church traditions. We are very grateful to all those who participated. Some of their comments appear throughout the material to encourage further thought. Some individuals have shared their personal experiences of encountering angels, and these have also been included. We were truly amazed how many people within such a small sample claimed to have had angelic experiences.

The ANGELS menu approach

Whenever you decide to use ANGELS, feel free to select and adapt the material to suit yourself or your group or congregation. Think of ANGELS more as a menu (choose which parts make the best meal for you) than as a recipe (make sure you have all the ingredients and the right amounts and follow the directions in order).

The material aims to be varied, recognising the many different ways people learn and think, and it's written from the understanding that people are at different stages in their relationship with God. So no previous knowledge of the Bible is assumed, though there will be opportunities to share from existing understanding. However, the material would be just as valuable with a group of mature believers as with a group of new Christians or enquirers.

The material is organised under a number of headings, such as:

Getting started	**Getting creative**
Bible encounter	**Taking it further**
Background notes	**Prayer response**

Hopefully, these are all self-explanatory. If you are a group or church leader you will know your members well enough to select activities and spend appropriate amounts of time on each to achieve a helpful balance of interaction, discovery, study and prayer. In order to cut down preparation time many activities are supported by photocopiable pages.

Towards the back of the book you will find some sections called **Personal Journey**. If you are working through the material on your own this will be a key section to look at. If you are working in a group, this provides some optional 'take-home' material which will enable you to build on the group times and add width and depth to your exploration. If your group does use the **Personal Journey** activity, do make sure there is opportunity to share insights gained at the start of every session after the first.

 After the first session most people had not managed all of the readings in Personal Journey, but found those that they had done were thought-provoking. It continued to be an option which people dipped into once or twice in between sessions.

Just a word about **Background notes**. If you are leading a group through the material, this will equip you to lead discussion times. As an option, you could summarise the notes for the rest of the group if you have time, but we don't see the need for you to read out the notes aloud in their entirety.

On your own?

If you are using ANGELS on your own, the indispensable sections of the material are **Bible encounter** and **Personal Journey**. But, depending on the time you have, many of the other activities can also be done solo. If you have Internet access, we encourage you to investigate some of the art images available online mentioned in the book, and indeed to spend time researching more widely. You will also be able to enjoy reading the book extracts and personal angel encounters, and activities such as the timeline and the song writing. Allow your creativity full rein! And do enter into as many of the prayer activities as you can.

The Oriel trilogy

Oriel's Diary, *Oriel's Travels* and *Oriel in the Desert* are a best-selling trilogy written by north west London vicar Robert Harrison and published by Scripture Union. If you have not discovered these novels, we warmly recommend them. They are fictionalised accounts supposedly written by one Oriel, an archangel gifted in administration. Oriel recounts the life of Jesus (in *Oriel's Diary*, based on Luke's gospel), Paul (in *Oriel's Travels*, rooted in Acts) and Moses (in *Oriel in the Desert*, using Exodus) from his unique heavenly viewpoint. A couple of extracts are given in ANGELS for you to use and enjoy. But if you are a group leader you may want to buy some copies of the books to share around or to recommend your group members to get the books for themselves. As well as being hugely entertaining they are very thought-provoking and certainly helped us to see angels in a whole new light!

Advance preparation

Some of the activities will need a little advance preparation:

Angels of power

— It will be helpful if someone researches some information about a part of the Christian church where persecution is happening. A good starting point would be a visit to the website of *Christianity Solidarity Worldwide* or that of a similar organisation.

— You will need gummed paper strips and pens to make prayer paper chains.

— Photocopies of or Internet access to images of the *Angel of the North*.

— Photocopies of the *Oriel's Travels* extract.

Angels of protection

— Prepare for an 'angelic feast'. This could have a Christmas or Thanksgiving theme or something different.

— Photocopies of one of the prayers.

— Photocopies of or access to images of Jacob Epstein's sculpture of *Jacob and the Angel* (kept at Tate Britain art gallery in London).

Angels of praise

— Materials for craft activities.

— Photocopies of the acrostic poem outline.

— Photocopies of or access to an image of *Michael's Victory over the Devil* by Jacob Epstein from the west wall of Coventry Cathedral.

 **Angels of proclamation**

— Materials for craft activities.

— Photocopies of the *Oriel's Diary* extract.

— Photocopies of or access to images of Rublev's *Icon of the Trinity* or El Greco's *Annunciation*.

Other resources

As well as those listed above, the following will be of interest to anyone wanting to explore the topic more:

Philip Pullman's *Northern Lights* trilogy

DVD of Mel Gibson's film *Signs*

Any collection of Christmas card images of angels

Although not directly referred to, these books would be useful extra reading:

Martin Israel, *Angels – Messengers of Grace,* London: SPCK, 1995.

Peter Williams, *The Case for Angels,* Carlisle: Paternoster, 2002.

Stephen F Noll, *Angels of Light, Powers of Darkness*, IVP, 1998.

B J Oropeza, *99 Answers to Questions about Angels, Demons and Spiritual Warfare,* IVP, 1997.

Bob Hartman, *Angels, Angels All Around*, Lion Hudson, 2004.

And there are some additional Scripture Union publications listed on page 64 for further study.

ANGELS OF POWER – GOD'S TASKFORCE

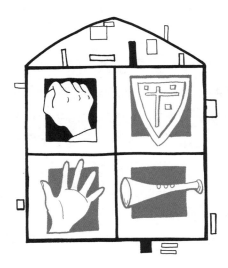

Purpose:

To explore the idea of angels as powerful agents doing God's will; revealing the mystery of God's creation and demonstrating the power of God himself; forever present and able to act at his command.

Getting started

When at night I go to sleep
Fourteen angels watch do keep;
Two my head are guarding,
Two my feet are guiding;
Two are on my right hand,
Two are on my left hand,
Two who warmly cover
Two who o'er me hover,
Two to whom 'tis given
To guide my steps to heaven.

from Humperdink's opera, *Hansel and Gretel*, often used as a lullaby

After reading this out, spend a few minutes discussing how much group members know about or have experience of angels. A song from childhood? Popular iconography? A literary reference? A personal experience? A Bible story?

 We had a very enlightening and free-flowing introductory discussion.

A whole range of stuff came out. We talked about everything from *Angel Delight* desserts to memories of Christmases from our childhoods!

 What expectation do group members have of angels being present in their own lives? In the world at large?

 We concluded that we had very little expectation of angels and our images of them were rather powerless, childish, ineffective, like the fairy on the Christmas tree.

Bible encounter

An angel rescues Peter from prison – Acts 12:1–19

Read this Bible passage aloud in a contemporary version such as the *Contemporary English Version*, *The Message* (in which the angel releases Peter to be 'free as the breeze'!) or the *New Living Translation*. Or read it as a drama, with a cast of five or more: a narrator, Peter, the angel, the believers. A simple script using the CEV is provided on page 18.

Background notes

The early church was under pressure both spiritually and politically (see especially Acts 4,5). Dark forces were seeking to crush the infant church. At this stage Peter was the acknowledged leader and a lightning rod for attack. He was now powerless in prison and the early church didn't know what to do. But they did pray.

Political and spiritual power are linked. The Jewish Council, the Sanhedrin, sought to exercise both. These Jewish leaders were fearful of losing their positions of influence and anxious about the popular unrest erupting all around them. Peter had been responsible for a very public healing in Christ's name, followed by an extended sermon explaining what had taken place (Acts 3). Acts 4:1–22 tells the story of how the Jewish council arrested Peter and John, interrogated them, threatened them and were astounded by their boldness and eloquence. When Peter and John reported back to the church, their fellow believers showed the same defiance as they prayed (Acts 4:23–31).

At no point did these early believers ask God to give them an easy life or to stop what he was doing. They asked God to carry on his work, and the place where they were praying was shaken (Acts 4:31). Acts 5 describes how the opposition moved from threats to outright persecution. By chapter 12 it is no surprise, then, to find that King Herod has ordered some killings and arrests in an attempt to dampen down the vigorous growth of the first Christians. What better than to arrest the ringleader and throw him into prison?

Peter's situation would appear to be completely hopeless. And yet, he managed to fall fast asleep (12:6). *The Message* describes him as sleeping like a baby! What stops people sleeping well? How was it then that Peter could sleep?

 God's angel comes with power into this situation (12:7–10). How would you describe the angel's actions?

 What evidence is there of the angel's sheer power? How does that contrast with the power exercised by King Herod and the religious authorities?

 Curiously enough, when Peter appears at Mary's house, people thought it might be Peter's *angel* rather than him personally (12:15). Does this necessarily suggest that we might be assigned a particular 'guardian angel' to look after us? (This is examined more if you look at Matthew 18:6–11, see page 51, so don't spend too long on this.)

When you are discussing angels, remember to let the Bible shape your thinking, rather than popular opinion!

Taking it further

Look up the very similar story in Acts 16:16–40 where Paul and Silas were arrested and thrown into prison just as Peter was in Acts 12. Paul and Silas were saved by an earthquake which scared the life out of the jailer and led to their release. There are real similarities between what happened in each situation, but this time no angel is mentioned.

 Is it possible that angels are at work, unseen, in the earthquake? We can never know, of course, but what do you think? Think again about the different powers (the authorities', God's) at work here.

If needed, there are additional passages in **Personal Journey** which expand the theme of the power of angels.

Living it today

 How aware are we of the spiritual battle in our lives? Or in other people's lives? Or in our local church? Or in the church nationally? Or in the church throughout the world?

 People generally agreed that there might be an awful lot of angelic activity going on that we are ignorant about. One or two talked about the Peretti novels which had influenced their thinking … made them more aware of angels.

In recent years the novels of Frank Peretti have become very popular with many Christians. They depict a society where supernatural happenings are very common and both angels and demons (fallen angels) are very active. It is very important to bear in mind that these are *fictional* accounts. They contain many details and perspectives which are imaginary and have little clear basis in scripture. This is one of those points at which it is absolutely essential to be guided by scripture and not by popular literature, however good the story might be. In fact the Bible doesn't give us many details about angels even though they appear a fair amount.

Getting creative

The angelic viewpoint

Read aloud the extract from *Oriel's Travels* on page 19 which tells the story of Peter's release from prison from a different viewpoint.

Oriel's Travels tells the story of the early church from the perspective of an archangel called Oriel who is in charge of administration in heaven. To fully enjoy this brief extract you need to know the 'cast':

— God the Father is known as 'the Boss'

— The Holy Spirit is known as 'the Director'

— Maff is one of Oriel's angel assistants

Note: This activity could be used as an introduction to the **Bible encounter,** to talk about what was happening to the early believers at this time. Use the **Background notes** to guide the discussion.

Believers under pressure

Explore situations of pressured or powerless or disenfranchised believers in different parts of the world today. This needs advance preparation of some information taken from literature or the websites of such organisations as:

— Christian Solidarity Worldwide (www.csw.org.uk.)

— Christian Freedom International (www.christianfreedom.org)

— Christians in Crisis (www.christiansincrisis.net)

— International Christian Concern (www.persecution.org)

— Open Doors (www.opendoorsuk.org.uk)

Make use of maps, photos/pictures and newspaper cuttings to prompt you to pray.

 The idea of angels being involved in upholding Christians under pressure stimulated our prayer.

Advent prayer ring

Make a simple advent ring by sticking five candles into half a large raw potato, arranging four candles around one central one, and securing on a strong, flat base. Decorate with holly, pine cones or tinsel. One explanation for the traditional use of the Advent ring is that the candles stand for the prophets, the Bible, John the Baptist and Mary, with Jesus in the centre. If you are using this material in the four-week Advent approach to Christmas, light candles every time you come to your prayer time – one for the first week, two for the second and so on.

Prayer response

Prayer paper chains

On gummed paper strips write prayer requests for individuals, your church, your church community, your locality, asking for spiritual power to be released into difficult situations. Encourage people to pray with great expectation. If God could send an angel to rescue Peter from prison, why can't he respond similarly in answer to your prayers?

Pray in twos or threes or altogether, with single sentence prayers, as appropriate, from your paper strips, then stick them together in chains and hang them up.

 The host couple for our group was happy to make the chains part of their Christmas decorations. We left some strips blank for the children in the house to add their own prayer requests and they enjoyed sharing in this activity. We referred to these chains over the next few weeks every time we came to pray and even added to them.

 Pray too for any special outreach events that your church is planning in the next few weeks.

Christmas and New Year are extremely busy times for church leaders and they will appreciate a commitment from you or your group to pray in this way.

Angel conversation challenge

Encourage people to talk to their colleagues, neighbours, family or friends, asking them what they think about angels. If you know someone from another faith, find out what they believe about angels. Talking about how you are part of a group or church looking at what the Bible says and people believe about angels is a natural opener to a conversation. Obviously, make sure you ask questions with genuine interest to find out. If you look at the trinkets for sale in gift shops or the titles in the 'mind, body, spirit' section of your local bookshop you will realise that there is a lot of interest in the topic of angels, so it may well be that most people you speak to will have views that they are willing to talk about with you. This could lead on to some thought-provoking conversations.

If you take up this challenge and are working through this material with others, be sure to report back at the next session and pray for each other and your contacts.

 In the week after this first session, two members of our group got talking with Muslim colleagues about what they believed about angels, stimulated by the group discussion. Both conversations were very enlightening and provided a very natural opportunity to talk about what Christians believe.

Spend a week with the Angels...

...is the invitation on a contact postcard for churches to use in outreach. Attractively designed, the double postcard has thought-provoking words and a freepost section offering a pack of seven Angels cards from Christian Enquiry Agency.

For more information go to www.christianity.org.uk.

The artist's view

The *Angel of the North* is possibly the most well-known contemporary icon of an angel. It is, in fact, the largest angel sculpture in the world, with a wingspan of 54 metres and a height of 20 metres – the equivalent of four double-decker buses! It speaks to those travelling to Gateshead in the north of England of welcome and power. You can track down some images by typing 'Angel of the North' into Google.

Antony Gormley, who created the *Angel of the North* sculpture, said, 'It is important to me that the angel is rooted in the ground – the complete antithesis of what an angel is, floating about in the ether. It has an air of mystery....The angel has three functions – firstly a historic one to remind us that below this site, coal miners worked in the dark for 200 years; secondly, to grasp hold of the future expressing our transition from the industrial to the information age; lastly, to be a focus for our hopes and fears.'

 How far does that reflect the powerful images of angels you have encountered using this material so far?

 I downloaded an image of this from a website and showed it on the screen of a laptop. Everyone knew about the sculpture and some had actually driven past it. It prompted some interesting discussion, the sort that we don't usually have in our home group.

 Everyone seemed to have a strong opinion about the *Angel of the North* – some loved it, others loathed it! We had a great discussion about what it had to say about what people today think about angels.

Real experience

RESCUE IN THE AUSTRALIAN OUTBACK

It was about 3am and we were on an overnight journey in Australia. The night sky sparkled with the millions of stars you can only see when away from city lights. We had been driving on a deserted highway for quite a few hours. As the children slept in the back seat, my wife and I were keeping a wary eye out for wild animals. We'd already seen emus, kangaroos and wild pigs. A collision with any of these would cause quite a bit of damage and even serious injury.

Suddenly, what we had feared happened. A kangaroo bounded out of nowhere and the car slammed into it with an enormous thud. The successive thumps indicated it had gone under the front wheel, the back wheel and finally the trailer we were towing. The trio in the back seat woke up in alarm and said in unison, 'What was that?'

We surveyed the damage to the car and realised we couldn't continue as there were bits of the car hanging off! Here we were, 450 miles due west of Brisbane, stranded in the outback, miles from anywhere, with a buckled car. We hadn't seen any other vehicles for hours.

We were standing around in confusion, when we became aware that coming from the same direction as we had driven, were some bright lights. As they came closer, they revealed themselves to be two huge and slow-moving road trains. These brightly-lit monsters pulled up in the middle of the highway with their engines rumbling. Two burly drivers descended from the cabins and, after surveying our plight, they fetched giant torches and various tools and proceeded to make our car drivable again.

We thanked them profusely. As they drove away I couldn't help wondering where they had come from. We had passed no other traffic on this lonely road. As if to answer my silent thoughts, my wife said, 'They were angels! Not terribly good-looking, but wonderful angels none the less!'

Drama script: An angel rescues Peter from prison

Narrator: King Herod caused terrible suffering for some members of the church. He ordered soldiers to cut off the head of James, the brother of John. When Herod saw that this pleased the Jewish people, he had Peter arrested during the Festival of Thin Bread. He put Peter in jail and ordered four squads of soldiers to guard him. Herod planned to put him on trial in public after the festival.

The night before Peter was to be put on trial, he was asleep and bound by two chains. A solider was guarding him on each side, and two other soldiers were guarding the entrance to the jail. Suddenly an angel from the Lord appeared, and light flashed around in the cell. The angel poked Peter in the side and woke him up.

Angel: Quick! Get up!

Narrator: The chains fell off his hands.

Angel: Get dressed and put on your sandals.

Narrator: Peter did what he was told.

Angel: Now put on your coat and follow me.

Narrator: Peter left with the angel, but he thought everything was only a dream. They went past the two groups of soldiers, and when they came to the iron gate to the city, it opened by itself. They went out and were going along the street, when all at once the angel disappeared.

Peter now realised what had happened.

Peter: I am certain that the Lord sent his angel to rescue me from Herod and from everything the Jewish leaders planned to do to me.

Narrator: Then Peter went to the house of Mary, the mother of John whose other name was Mark. Many of the Lord's followers had come together there and were praying.

Peter knocked on the gate, and a servant named Rhoda came to answer. When she heard Peter's voice, she was too excited to open the gate. She ran back into the house and said that Peter was standing there.

Believers: You're mad!

Narrator: But she kept saying that it was Peter.

Believers: It must be his angel!

Narrator: But Peter kept on knocking, until finally they opened the gate. They saw him and were completely amazed.

Rescuing Peter

In Heaven

'I'm glad you came so promptly. I would like you to rescue Peter for me.'

I was somewhat taken aback. I had knocked on my Boss's door armed with the question, *What are you planning to do about Peter?* I wasn't expecting to be part of the plan.

'How?' I asked.

'I'm sure you can work something out,' he replied. 'If you can release all the resurrected captives of Death from a small tomb, you should be able to rescue one man from a Jewish prison.'

I went straight to my office and called Maff.

John Mark's house, Jerusalem - that night

Maff and I checked out the prison where Peter was being held and worked out the simplest route from Peter's cell to freedom. We then worked our way back though the labyrinth of steps, tunnels and dark cells, putting everyone into a deep sleep. Peter was already deeply asleep. I tried to rouse him several times without success.

When I had used the whole spectrum of Angelic speech, from gentle whisper to anxious yell, Maff said, 'You'll have to get physical with him.' He was right.

I thinned my Angelic being to something near the shadowy existence of humans and called out to Peter's ears rather than his mind. I had a small measure of success; he gave a loud snort and started snoring loudly. Unexpectedly, another Angelic light appeared in the cell. I turned round to see Gabriel watching me, an amused grin on his face.

'Do you want any help?' he asked.

'No thank you.'

I returned my attention to the sleeping form of Peter and gave him a firm shove in the side. It worked. He opened his eyes and looked straight at me with dumbstruck horror.

Gabriel cheered.

'Quick, get up!' I told Peter, concerned that the guards might be woken by Gabriel's racket. Then, to Maff I said, 'Take those chains off his arms.'

That done, I handed Peter the clothes and sandals that were in a heap on the damp floor. 'Put these on,' I said. He was still staring at me with his mouth hanging open.

Maff handed me a cloak that one of the guards had been using as a blanket. 'This is Peter's, too,' he said.

I had to physically haul the burly fisherman to his feet. 'Put this round you and follow me.' I turned around to discover that Michael had joined Gabriel.

'Well done, Oriel' Gabriel called with amused delight.

Michael added, 'The way you barked out those orders, we'll make a soldier of you yet.'

Maff swung open the heavy wooden door and I led Peter out of his cell. Peter seemed dazed. I don't think he had much clue about what was actually happening. Past two sets of sleeping guards we eventually came to a heavy metal gate, again opened by Maff. It led directly into a deserted street.

I walked with Peter, still in something of a dream, to the end of the road. Maff called to me from above the houses, 'Come on Oriel, hurry up. He's out of the prison now and he's lived here ten years. He doesn't need a tour guide.'

I looked at the man, a string of dribble now swinging from his lower lip. He needed something. I resorted to a method I've seen humans using on one another and gave Peter a firm slap on the cheek. Then I resumed my usual form, joined Maff, and we returned to Paul's lodgings at John Mark's house where a large crowd of disciples were hard at prayer. They were imploring my Boss for Peter's freedom. I told Paul that their prayers had already been answered but he was too distracted to hear.

I spoke to the Director, 'Can't you tell him that his request is received, understood and granted?'

'He's not listening.'

Maff and I waited as the roomful of Heaven's children pleaded desperately to their divine Father with such energy that not one of them could hear his reply. After a while there was a knock at the door. It was Peter. Nobody responded. Some decided that their prayers were more important than any visitor who might be knocking in the middle of the night, others were afraid that the knocking might be Herod's soldiers, come to arrest them too. Peter knocked again, harder. Those who feared arrest redoubled their prayers. Eventually one of the household's servants, a girl called Rhoda, took it upon herself to find out who was at the door.

'It's me. Peter!'

Rhoda ran back into the main room and declared, 'Peter's outside the door!'

'Don't be stupid,' came the reply. 'Peter's in prison. That's why we're all praying for him.'

'But I recognised his voice. It's him,' the poor girl insisted.

'It must be his Angel guardian,' someone suggested.

Rhoda stared around the crowded room, now quiet, searching for someone who might believe her. Then a voice boomed from behind her, 'For goodness sake, will somebody let me in.'

Stunned silence. No one moved. Finally, Paul spoke up.

'Well, let him in then.'

When Peter was finally admitted he told the astounded gathering, 'It's easier to get out of Herod's prison than it is to get in here.'

An extract from *Oriel's Travels* © Robert Harrison published by Scripture Union and used with permission.

2
ANGELS OF PROTECTION – GOD'S SECRET AGENTS

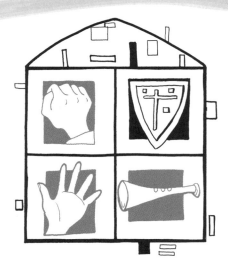

Purpose:

To explore the idea of angels as ever-present protectors, demonstrating God's mysterious commitment to the safety of his people on a day-to-day basis.

Getting started

Read the following story aloud and invite group members to discuss their experiences of angels as protectors. You could also read any other of the **Real experience** stories – you'll find them listed on the contents page; or photocopy them all and distribute them around smaller groups for discussion.

Real experience

SEVENTEEN HEAVENLY GUARDS

Two women missionaries who ran a small dispensary on the borders of China and Tibet were taking supplies by mule from the railhead to their home. One of the mules went lame and they couldn't make their shelter by nightfall so had to sleep rough under a big rockface. The next day they went on to their home, none the worse.

Several months later a man suffering from knife wounds came for help and when they had treated him he said that he and some other men had planned to kill them at their bivouac until they counted no fewer than 17 large soldiers acting as sentries.

Some months later the two women had a letter from home saying the church's regular missionary prayer meeting had felt particularly concerned to pray about them on a particular evening – which turned out to be the night when they were out in the open. The letter went on to mention there had been a good turnout for the prayer meeting – 17 people.

Bible encounter

Elisha and the army of the Lord – 2 Kings 6:8–23

Background notes

The word 'angel' is mentioned more than 250 times in the Bible! No fewer than 34 of the Bible's 66 books talk about angels.

Generally speaking we are unaware of the lengths God goes to in keeping us from harm. We pray in the Lord's Prayer, 'deliver us from evil', but inevitably tend to take God's protection for granted. Most of us weren't run down by a lorry as we made our way to the office or to the shopping centre this week. Nor were we mugged by a gang of thieves carrying knives. God looks after us and we normally don't even recognise it. This is true in the normal run of everyday events – but it is also true when we are faced with major crises.

And it was true for Israel's army facing attack from their enemies. The historical books of 1 and 2 Kings tell the story of the kings of Israel following King David. Under Solomon, David's son, the kingdom was united. But after Solomon the kingdom divided into two: the northern kingdom of Israel and the southern kingdom of Judah. Israel was frequently in conflict with the surrounding nations. Sometimes, maybe, it was Israel's fault. Often Israel provoked a foreign power and suffered the consequences. More frequently it was that, as is common in our big, bad world, people wanted what others had. At this time in its history, Israel often had particular problems with the northern neighbour, Syria (sometimes called 'Aram').

As things stand politically, there is an uneasy peace between Israel and Aram/Syria. Israel's king is a weak king. Sometimes he treats the prophets very well; at other times he treats them badly. As one of the descendants of the 'House of Ahab' he is under God's judgment for all the wicked things that have been done in their name (1 Kings 21:20–26).

If anyone knows anything about the historical background of this story, encourage them to share their knowledge. If not, summarise the notes above. A map would locate Syria and Israel, and Dothan itself.

Read 2 Kings 6:8–23 aloud. If you want to dramatise it, a simple script using the text of *The Message* is on page 25. You will need a cast of six: a narrator, the king of Aram, the king of Israel, Elisha, a servant and an officer.

 This story is full of surprises! Three questions are asked in verses 11, 15 and 21. Did those who asked the questions expect the answers they got?

 Can you imagine this scene when the angelic force is revealed? How would you describe their activity?

Living it today

 What does this story show us about the nature of a spiritual realm beyond our 'normal' experience of life? How does this spiritual world impact the material world?

 How might appreciating the existence of this spiritual world influence the way we think about our lives?

What is the role of angelic forces at work in situations of war today? What about other situations of danger?

 People were very unsure about whether angelic hosts are to be found in today's battlefields.

 Look at Ephesians 6:10–20. How do you understand Paul's description of 'the spiritual forces of evil in the heavenly realms'?

If needed, there are additional passages in **Personal Journey** which expand the theme of the angels in the role of protectors.

 Looking at Hebrews 13:2, discuss the things that motivate us to offer hospitality to others. How might our current concerns about 'stranger danger' conflict with this biblical instruction to entertain strangers? What insight does this verse offer into how angels operate?

Read Hebrews 1:14 and Matthew 18:10,11

 In the light of these Bible verses, do we each have guardian angels? What do they do? Can we communicate with them? Does each person have their very own named angel? See also page 51 for more discussion of Matthew 18 and the question of guardian angels.

Background notes

Some people think that what Jesus says in the Matthew verses refers to 'guardian angels'. It may be a comforting idea to think that we each have our own angel. But overall it would be hard to argue that the Bible really supports this, since the main thrust of Bible teaching is that the task of all God's angels is to serve all God's people. Calvin's view was: 'The care of each one of us is not the task of one angel only, but all with one consent watch over our salvation.'

Getting creative

Thanksgiving for protection

If you are meeting in a small group for your ANGELS experience, it would be worth having a meal together on at least one occasion. If you are in Advent, you could have an American-style Thanksgiving meal (turkey, cranberry sauce, mashed potato and pumpkin pie) – which traditionally takes place on the fourth Thursday of November – a celebration begun by the early settlers in America commemorating their survival and the fact that God had kept and protected them in their first year.

An angelic feast

Alternatively, you might like to create an angelic feast. The food could reflect some of the characteristics of angels such as **surprising**: for example, baked Alaska (ice cream, wrapped in meringue and baked in the oven) or something served in sweet and sour sauce or something **strong** (in taste) or something **light and airy** (a creamy concoction). Or you could provide food

that has 'angels' in its name, such as angels on horseback (bacon wrapped around oysters, served on toast – an acquired taste maybe!), angel cake, *Angel Delight* dessert, angel hair pasta/capellini (extra fine; Delia Smith uses it with prawns, shrimps, herbed ricotta and chicken!), angelica (used in fruit cake). You could even invent your own angel menu! Have fun!

During the meal, thank God for the way he protects and provides for us.

Personal timeline

Photocopy the timeline provided on page 26.

Ask everyone to draw a journey line of their life, with all its ups and downs. Include birth, early childhood, school years, young adulthood, middle years, retiring years, as appropriate. Put in symbols along the line to mark significant events – for example, a star when you came to faith or had a special experience of God, a cross for the death of a loved one, a cloud for a time of difficulty, a tear shape for a sad time. Encourage people to be creative about how they 'draw' their life.

In pairs, share your completed timeline with each other, describing how God and his angels have protected you along the way, even though probably you couldn't see them.

 There was a real buzz and enthusiasm to share insights...

Then call the group back together and invite discussion on this question: Are we more protected/ less exposed to harmful risks than previous generations? Some of the older members of the group may have some helpful observations. If you conclude that we are more 'cosseted', does that mean we are more or less open to perceiving angelic appearances?

Prayer response

Encourage short prayers of thanks for how God has protected us in the past.

Pray for preparations being made for Christmas by your church, especially for outreach events. Ask God to protect all those involved and the events themselves.

 Our church leader was so encouraged that we were praying for the Christmas preparations each time we met.

Give out photocopies of one of the prayers on page 27 to say together, then take away and keep.

 Don't forget to continue using your Advent ring during the prayer time if you have one.

The artist's view

In Tate Britain you will find Epstein's huge sculpture *Jacob and the Angel*, made out of alabaster and weighing 2500 kg. Look up Epstein on the Tate Britain website (www.tate.org.uk) for a view of this. You may be able to look at the image on a laptop or download and make photocopies of the image while someone reads the account from Genesis 32:22–32.

During the early 1930s Epstein read and re-read Genesis and created a series of watercolours of the Old Testament stories. This story of Jacob and the angel fascinated him, perhaps partly because his own first name was Jacob. His sculpture, finished in 1940, is based on a watercolour he did in 1932.

In Genesis 27 we read that Jacob tricked his father Isaac into giving him the birthright belonging to Esau, his elder brother. Later, in Genesis 32:22–32, at a crisis time in his life, Jacob wrestled throughout the night with an unknown assailant, described as a man, but revealed as an angel and a messenger from God. *Or was it God himself?*

The sculpture portrays the angel as supporting Jacob, who hangs limply in his arms – but the two are somehow inseparable. The angel seems to be almost squeezing the life out of Jacob who has his eyes closed and his head thrown back. Notice the sheer strength and power of the angel and the protective way he holds onto Jacob.

 What does this portrayal of an angel tell us about people's perceptions of angels?

His Dark Materials – **Philip Pullman**

Philip Pullman's highly acclaimed *Dark Materials* trilogy, written for children and adults, presents a world without God and takes a very sceptical swipe at the Church as an institution. While some people view the books as a triumph of imaginative writing, others are wary of an agenda of attack on the Christian Church.

The novels are peopled by all sorts of 'beings', but one of the most interesting creations is that of 'daemons'. These are beings, one assigned to each person, which everyone has with them; almost a physical representation or extension of their personality, to complement and accompany them. A child's 'daemon' is not settled in its final form and can change. By reading the first few chapters of *Northern Lights* you will grasp the concept of 'daemons'.

 How far do you think Pullman's 'daemons' are like popular understanding about guardian angels? From his atheistic perspective, would he see an angel simply as an alter ego? It is interesting that he creates all sorts of other spiritual beings too!

Signs

If you haven't already seen the film, watch the video/DVD of *Signs* (Mel Gibson) which engages with the idea of unseen 'angelic' forces all around us.

 How much of Mel Gibson's ideas could a believer endorse?

 Would there be any merit in using the film as an evangelistic 'starter' for discussion with non-believers?

Drama script: Elisha and the army of the Lord – 2 Kings 6:8–23

Narrator:	One time when the king of Aram was at war with Israel, after consulting with his officers, he said:
K/Aram:	At a certain place, I want an ambush set.
Narrator:	Elisha, the holy man, sent a message to the king of Israel.
Elisha:	Watch out when you're passing this place, because Aram has set an ambush there.
Narrator:	So the king of Israel sent word concerning the place about which Elisha had warned him. This kind of thing happened all the time! The king of Aram was furious over all this. He called his officers together.
K/Aram:	Tell me, who is leaking information to the king of Israel? Who is this spy in our ranks?
Officer:	No, master. It's not any of us. It's Elisha the prophet in Israel. He tells the king of Israel everything you say, even what you whisper in your bedroom.
K/Aram:	Go and find out where he is. I'll send someone and capture him.
Narrator:	The report came back that he was in Dothan. Then the king dispatched horses and chariots, an impressive fighting force. They came by night and surrounded the city. Early in the morning Elisha's servant got up and went out. Surprise! Horses and chariots were surrounding the city! The young man exclaimed:
Servant:	Oh, master! What shall we do?
Elisha:	Don't worry about it – there are more on our side than on their side.
Narrator:	Then Elisha prayed:
Elisha:	O God, open his eyes and let him see.
Narrator:	The eyes of the young man were opened and he saw. A wonder! The whole mountainside was full of horses and chariots of fire surrounding Elisha! When the Arameans attacked, Elisha prayed to God:
Elisha:	Strike these people blind!
Narrator:	And God struck them blind, just as Elisha said. Then Elisha called out to them:
Elisha:	Not that way! Not this city! Follow me and I'll lead you to the man you're looking for.
Narrator:	And he led them into Samaria. As they entered the city, Elisha prayed:
Elisha:	O God, open their eyes so they can see where they are.
Narrator:	God opened their eyes. They looked around – they were trapped in Samaria! When the king of Israel saw them, he said to Elisha:
K/Israel:	Father, shall I massacre the lot?
Elisha:	Not on your life! You didn't lift a hand to capture them, and now you're going to kill them? No sir, make a feast for them and send them back to their master.
Narrator:	So he prepared a huge feast for them. After they ate and drank their fill he dismissed them. Then they returned home to their master. The raiding bands of Aram didn't bother Israel anymore.

Personal timeline

... he will command his angels concerning you to guard you in all your ways; they will lift you up in their hands, so that you will not strike your foot against a stone.

Psalm 91:11,12

1940 1945 1950 1955 1960 1965 1970 1975 1980 1985 1990 1995 2000 2005 2010

Prayer bookmarks

Alone with none but thee, my God, I journey on my way. What need I fear when thou art near, O King of night and day? More safe am I within thy hand Than if a host did round me stand.

St Columba

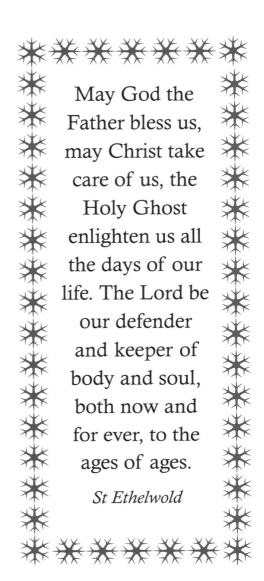

May God the Father bless us, may Christ take care of us, the Holy Ghost enlighten us all the days of our life. The Lord be our defender and keeper of body and soul, both now and for ever, to the ages of ages.

St Ethelwold

LIGHTEN OUR DARKNESS, WE BESEECH THEE, O LORD; AND BY THY GREAT MERCY DEFEND US FROM ALL PERILS AND DANGERS OF THIS NIGHT; FOR THE LOVE OF THY ONLY SON, OUR SAVIOUR JESUS CHRIST. AMEN.

The Book of Common Prayer

3
ANGELS OF PRAISE
– GOD'S WORSHIPPERS

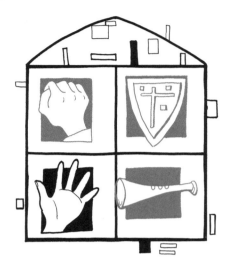

Purpose:

To explore the idea of angels as part of the whole of creation – natural and supernatural – worshipping God.

Getting started

Find a CD or tape of music that is focused upon worshipping God and listen to two or more songs.

OR

Sing some worship songs which are directed God-wards.

 Did anyone wonder whether the angels were joining in? If not, why not? If so, why was this? Who else might be joining in?

 ## Bible encounter

John sees worship in heaven – Revelation 4, 5

Background notes

Angels are part of God's wonderful creation and reflect his glory in many ways, not least in their beauty and power. It is hardly surprising that they often provoke responses of terror or worship. Sometimes they have to discourage worship of themselves – since worship should only be directed towards God.

John Calvin wrote in his *Institutes of the Christian Religion*:

Surely, since the splendour of the divine majesty shines in them, nothing is easier for us than to fall down, stupefied, in adoration of them, and then to attribute to them that which is owed to God alone. Even John in Revelation confesses that this happened to him, but at the same time he adds that this answer came to him [19:10; 22:8,9]: 'Do not do it! I am a fellow-servant with you ... Worship God.'

The book of Revelation has provoked many weird and wonderful interpretations. People frequently begin reading it with a lot of presuppositions. Chapter 1 simply describes John's extraordinary experience as a prisoner on the island of Patmos, when he has a vivid vision of the Lord Jesus Christ. Jesus appeared to him to deliver messages to seven churches situated in what is now western Turkey. When John has received these messages, he has another vision of the worship of all of creation in heaven.

John's vision is of all orders of creation – seen and unseen – worshipping God. One of the least considered aspects of redemption is that God intends to redeem all that he has created, with humanity as a crucial part of this. Romans 8 explores the implications of this to the whole of creation. Paul starts out by affirming that Christians are God's adopted children (verses 12–17). He then goes on to explain how the whole of creation has been waiting for humanity to repent (verses 18–25). Paul tells us that creation groans in longing to see the fulfilment of all of God's plans. It is easy to forget that when Adam and Eve fell and sin entered God's world, the whole of creation was damaged as well and became less fruitful (Genesis 3:14–19).

 From reading Romans 8:12–17, what does Paul say for certain about what God has done for us, despite the death-bringing damage of sin?

 Life now, before we go to be with God forever, is full of uncertainties. What does Paul say in Romans 8:18–25 about the present condition of creation – and us as part of that?

It is hardly surprising, then, that Revelation offers us a picture of all of creation worshipping God together. That certainly includes angelic beings!

 Revelation 4 and 5 are similar but also different. What are the differences? What is missing from chapter 4?

 How many different groups of figures are there in chapter 5 and who might they each represent in John's vision?

 Angels only come into the picture in 5:11. Why do you think they are there at all?

If needed, there are additional passages in **Personal Journey** which expand the theme of the praise of angels.

Getting creative

Acrostic praise poems

Write a song or a poem celebrating God's redemption of all creation and creation's response. It could be done as an acrostic, using the letters of ANGELS or PRAISE. Photocopiable templates are provided for you on pages 33 and 34.

Share your contributions. Someone musical might like to set one or more to music. Or the poem could be illustrated, perhaps with a scene from Revelation 4 or 5.

> People really got into this and produced some great art. The acrostic idea worked well. It helped that we were meeting in a house where there were young children with plenty of craft stuff.

> Creative ideas get you thinking in a different way and got us away from having the usual discussion which generally begins with me, as the leader, asking a question.

Here is a great poem produced by someone in our trial groups:

A cross the galaxies

N earing God's beloved orb,

G athering angels approached

E xpecting the awesome miracle,

L ighting up that night with glory,

S inging, Son of God, Saviour's born.

Angel song samplers

An alternative activity would be to illustrate a verse from a song about angels praising God. Verses which work well would be:

— verse 4 of 'Praise, My Soul, the King of Heaven'
— 'From the Squalor of a Borrowed Stable'
— 'Angels Voices ever Singing'
— 'Songs of Praise the Angels Sang'
— 'I Cannot Tell Why He Whom Angels Worship'
— 'Angels From the Realms of Glory'

You could place the verse inside a border and decorate with paint, felt-tips, glitter and glue, strips of silk or ribbons etc. A ready-made template is provided as an example on page 35.

 Can you think of other songs, hymns or carols which refer to angels? How many can people name? Revelation 4 and 5 themselves have been fruitful sources for many songs! What other Bible passages, if any, have formed the basis for these songs?

Prayer and praise response

Many hymn and song books give a scripture reference section at the back so that you can see the source Bible verses. Look there for any hymns or songs referring to Revelation 4 or 5. Spend time singing some of these, followed by a time of sharing in prayer and praise, offering your own words of gratitude to God for his holiness, his power, his glory; and for Jesus whose death makes him worthy to receive power, riches, wisdom, strength, honour, glory and praise. You could also make use of the poems and songs that have been written during the session; and if you are in Advent, why not select one or two favourite carols to sing?

 Don't forget to pray for the preparations for Christmas events that are planned for your church.

 Did anyone wonder if angels were joining in your praise? Compare your answers from the start of the session.

Taking it further

Orders of angels research project

This material can't possibly hope to say everything there is to say about angelic beings. Some people may want to take their knowledge a little bit further and what follows is some help in that direction. Much terminology relating to angels and heavenly creatures is unclear and very influenced by popular culture from biblical times to the present day.

Find out what you can about the various 'ranks' of angels by consulting a Bible encyclopaedia or dictionary. To get you started:

Cherubim (singular: cherub) are winged creatures, close to God, with feet, hands and often more than one face. Their tasks include guarding the tree of life (Genesis 3:24) and symbolically protecting the ark of the covenant (Exodus 25:18–22; Hebrews 9:5). They also transport the throne of God (Ezekiel 10). Other references include 2 Samuel 22:11; Psalm 18:10.

Seraphim are only mentioned in Isaiah 6. Like cherubim, they guard the throne of God. The word possibly comes from the Hebrew 'sarap' meaning 'to burn', which suggests their role was to purify.

Archangels are those angelic leaders who are especially close to God. Although only two are mentioned by name in the Bible (Michael and Gabriel) there are possibly two more of them (Raphael and Sariel or Uriel) though some traditions say there are seven and some ancient Jewish literature names even more. Mention of Raphael can be found in a book which is not in the usual canon of Scripture, called 1 Enoch (9:1). This book dates from around the time of the New Testament and, in common with a number of other Jewish writings of the time, it has a certain interest in heavenly realities and expands the information about angels a good deal.

Fallen angels are also assumed but are understandably not give much profile. See Job 4:18; Isaiah 14:12–15; Matthew 25:41; 2 Peter 2:4; Revelation 12:9.

If you have read any of the Oriel trilogy you will be aware of the author's fascinating ideas on the relationships between archangels, angels and fallen angels.

The artist's view

Download an image of the enormous bronze statue *St Michael's Victory over the Devil,* constructed by Sir Jacob Epstein in 1958 at the entrance of the new Coventry Cathedral. It constitutes a powerful symbol of the triumphant resurrection of the cathedral after wartime devastation. Epstein died in 1959 and did not live to see the mounting of his work of art.

 What do you understand about Epstein's view of the archangel from his statue?

 What can you discover about the archangel Michael from the Bible?

Note: Yet again, it is important to distinguish between what the Bible tells us about angelic beings (the truth, or rather *part* of the truth) and what impressions we gain from fiction or creative writing, paintings, sculptures etc. The artistic temperament has been drawn to the topic of angels and there are various imaginative elaborations, some closer to scripture than others.

Real experience

ANGELS AND THE OXFORD BUS

For our twenty-fifth wedding anniversary we were treating ourselves to a week's holiday on the island of Malta. Our son Jonathan, then 20, was staying at our home in Oxford on a college break, doing some temping work.

As I dozed on the plane I came to myself very abruptly. In my mind I had seen a picture of Jonathan, surrounded by four figures. Although the figures had no detail, I knew – somehow – that they were angels. What did this dream or vision mean? I had never experienced anything similar. I became quite anxious, imagining all sorts of things.

By the time we had touched down, collected our hire car and driven to our hotel at St Paul's Bay, it was dark. I felt I needed to phone home. Mobile phones were not widespread then and it took some time to work out how to buy an international phone card to use in the kiosk over the road from the hotel.

Eventually, I got through. Jonathan was amazed to hear from me. He had just returned from the hospital. Earlier that day he had been involved in an accident. Cycling along one of the main roads from the city centre he had been squeezed as a bus in front of him cut in to the kerb just in front of a parked car. The bus had clipped his bike and Jonathan was thrown into the road. He had been taken to hospital. He was suffering from concussion and a few cuts and bruises, but nothing worse, and had been discharged as long as a friend was able to stay with him overnight.

When I got home and saw his cycle helmet – completely split through – I was convinced that I had seen nothing less than a glimpse of four angels of protection as they surrounded my son at the time of his collision with the bus.

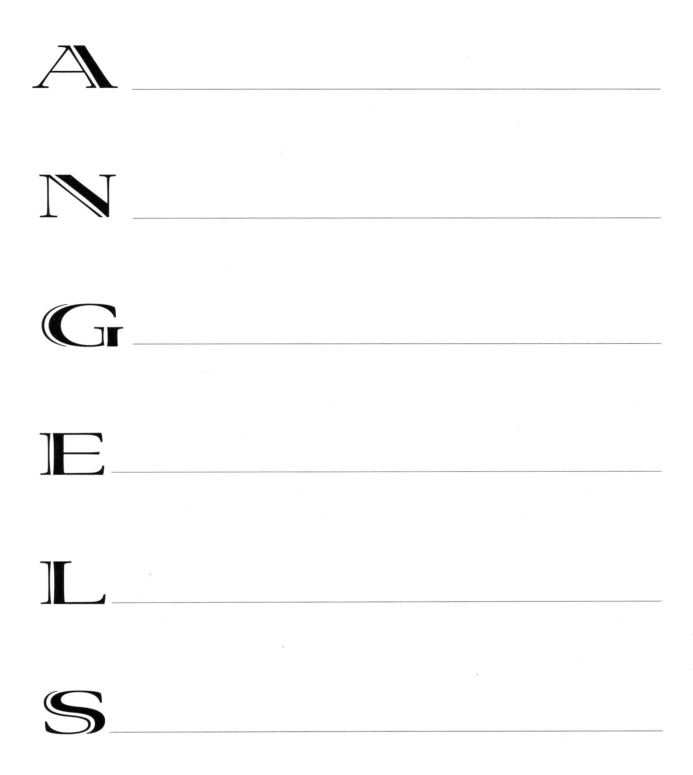

A _____

N _____

G _____

E _____

L _____

S _____

P

R

A

I

S

E

Angel voices ever singing
Round thy throne of light,
Angel harps for ever ringing,
Rest not day nor night;
Thousands only live to bless Thee,
And confess Thee Lord of might.

4
ANGELS OF PROCLAMATION
– GOD'S MESSENGERS

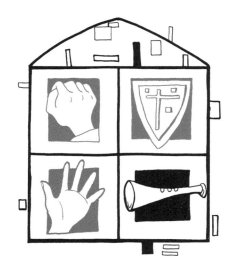

Purpose:

To explore the idea of angels as those entrusted with the words of God himself; God's intermediaries.

Getting started

Begin by singing a couple of worship songs (or carols if you are in Advent); and then pass around any Christmas cards collected by the group which portray angels.

 List and discuss adjectives (describing words) which relate to these images. Are the four aspects of angels mentioned in this material – power, protection, praise and proclamation – all represented?

Note: There may be other comments about how the pictures on the cards relate to the actual Christmas story! But that's another discussion.

 Everyone seemed to agree that the emasculation of the angels on our Christmas cards – often portrayed as feminine, fairy-like and cute – mirrored the emasculation of the churches and the way that the gospel is presented. The real Christmas story has been systematically robbed of its power, glory and immensity to become a pretty fable!

Alternatively, you could download an image of one of El Greco's *Annunciation* (more detail on page 41) and discuss how this artist presents the archangel.

Bible encounter

Gabriel comes to Mary – Luke 1:26–38

Background notes

Angels tend to become prominent at very special times in God's dealings with humanity. Matthew 1 and 2 focus on Joseph's experience at the time of the birth of Jesus. Joseph certainly needed some divine guidance and an angel actually appears to him three times, each time in a dream, with precise instructions as to what to do (Matthew 1:20–22; 2:13 and 2:19,20). Even the Magi received instructions (Matthew 2:12).

Luke tells the story very much from the perspective of Mary, the mother of Jesus. In the early part of Luke 1, however, it is Zechariah, the father of Jesus' cousin John the Baptist, who is the centre of attention. There are many points of similarity in the account of Gabriel's visit to Zechariah in Luke 1:8–20 when he announces his wife Elizabeth's pregnancy and Gabriel's visit to Mary later (Luke 1:26–38). Both Zechariah and Mary are simply going about their daily tasks, both are overwhelmed with fear, both are told that God is going to shatter the normal routines of their lives, both are told exactly what the significance of their forthcoming sons is to be, both utter a 'How on earth … !' sort of question (Luke 1:18,34) and Gabriel gives them both an answer. The difference is that Zechariah's questions implies scepticism, which Gabriel doesn't appreciate (Luke 1:19,20) and is struck dumb for his cheek! Mary, on the other hand, simply asks for clarification, which she receives. She is accepting and submissive to Gabriel's message.

There could, of course, be no more special occasion than the birth of God's Son. Certainly Mary needed all the preparation she could get! In Jewish literature Gabriel is especially associated with bringing messages.

 What are the similarities and what the differences between the two accounts: Luke 1:11–20 and 1:26–38. You could split into two groups with one group listing the key points that describe what happened to Zechariah and the other doing the same for Mary. Then compare notes.

 What was Mary's first reaction to Gabriel's words (Luke 1:29)? How would you describe her second reaction (verse 34)? And what about her third response (verse 38)?

 Notice that Gabriel doesn't just give a message and depart. He answers questions when they are appropriately put to him (not like Zechariah!). Why do you think this might be?

Taking it further

 Look at Genesis 18:1–15. Abraham's visitors may have been the Trinity. This is the view of the Orthodox tradition. Or they could be three angels. If they were angels, what does this say about angelic appearances? This was such a detailed message. At what point do you think Abraham discerned that these were no ordinary visitors? Hebrews 13:2 may be referring to this incident, in which case they must be angels. What similarities are there between this incident and the message that Gabriel has to deliver to both Zechariah and Mary?

If needed, there are additional passages in **Personal Journey** which expand the theme of the messenger role of angels.

Getting creative

Angel creation

Using a variety of craft materials, create your own angel, working on your own, in pairs, or in small groups. It could be a flat image, or – for the more ambitious – a three-dimensional one.

Useful materials include:

tissue paper	silver florist's wire
scraps of silk	feathers
wired wool	glitter
cotton wool	handmade paper
card	pieces of coloured felt
ribbon	tinsel

The end result could be a table decoration, a candle-holder, a poster to display in church, a bookmark or even a Christmas card.

 Often leaders just won't touch the creative ideas, thinking that people won't do it, think it is childish, or doesn't suit their learning style. It requires courageous leadership to introduce it. But for those who do take the risk, the benefits are often huge in terms of allowing people to explore the truth of God's Word in a different way and to do it together!

 One member made everyone in the group an angel using an old-fashioned clothes peg, sparkly pipe cleaners and a white feather. It was just great!

An angel for Skipton Baptist Church

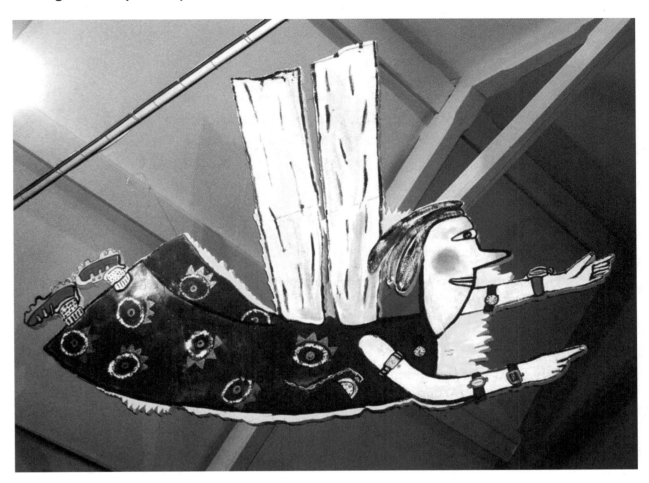

One of the trial groups using ANGELS were blessed with the artistic abilities of Chris Murray, who created this wonderful image of an angel in acrylic on a polystyrene panel 2.5 by 1.5 metres to hang in the church.

Chris recalls:

> The brief was to produce a temporary decoration depicting an angel, suspended from the ceiling and pointing to an existing wooden cross – illustrating the fact that, of all things, an angel's job is to point towards the pre-eminent Christ. The result was a not-too-serious blend of two kinds of information. Firstly: visionary detail from the Bible that immediately tell us the figure is an angel – wings and eyes (which appear as decoration on the robe). Secondly: some speculative imaginings from me, to provoke fresh thoughts about the subject of angels. A friend said he didn't like the way angels always looked effeminate hence the football boots, suggesting power exercised beautifully. The watches relate to the fact that an angel's life consists of meeting some pretty precise deadlines, probably across a multitude of time zones! I imagine angels are fascinated by time, not being defined by it as we are.

Drama

The story of Gabriel visiting Mary is usually seen from the point of view of Mary and God's wider plan. Using your imagination, create a dramatic presentation of Gabriel's preparation to visit Mary. Perhaps the archangel wonders about how to present himself, what to say and how to say it? Aim to convey a greater appreciation of the angelic task.

To start you off, on page 45 you will find an excerpt from *Oriel's Diary* which gives the archangel Oriel's viewpoint. Having read this, your task is to come up with a short drama from Gabriel's perspective.

> We did two dramas, one of Gabriel preparing to visit Zechariah and one of him preparing to visit Mary. They both used a boardroom planning meeting approach. They came out quite well with much laughter over Gabriel striking Zechariah dumb!

Alternatively, you could use the dramatic readings printed on pages 43 and 44 from that excellent resource, *The Dramatised Bible*. The first reading needs five voices; the second also needs five, but everyone else could join in with the angels' song.

 If your group gets really enthusiastic about this, consider offering it for presentation in an Advent or Christmas worship service.

Prayer response

Reflect on all the messages that are proclaimed by angels in the Christmas story – to Zechariah, Mary, the shepherds (Luke 1 and 2), the wise men and Joseph (Matthew 1 and 2). Ask each member of the group to think about one of these people and why they responded in the way that they did.

On a large sheet of paper write down phrases which sum up each character's response to God's message.

Then ask each member to identify a time when they felt God speaking to them. How did they respond? Invite a few people to share their reflections. Spend some time in prayer together, thanking God that he speaks to us.

 Make sure that at the end of this session you pray for your Christmas activities in church and all those involved in making them happen. Pray too for your community.

Conclude by singing 'O, Come Let Us Adore Him!' with the additional verses of 'For He Alone is Worthy' and 'We'll Give Him All the Glory'.

Alternatively, sing the whole carol of 'O, Come, All Ye Faithful' making the 'Sing, choirs of angels' verse as joyful as you can!

Living it today

The angels' commitment to proclaim the truth and wonder of God – Father, Son and Spirit – not only challenges us to consider our response to God's Word but also challenges us to be like the angels in proclaiming the truth about God to a world that does not acknowledge him.

Q How might you reach out into your geographical community or help each other to reach out into the different work and social communities where you each belong?

 If you are doing this series in Advent, Christmas provides many natural opportunities for outreach. (*Christmas Wrapped Up* is a Scripture Union resource with bags of ideas to think about: see page 64.)

If you are doing this series at another time of the year, what plans do you have to follow the example of the proclaiming angels? Find time to pray specifically for this.

The artist's view

Andrei Rublev painted his *Icon of the Trinity*, a representation of Abraham's three visitors, around 1410. Find an image of this on the Internet and see if it helps you decide if Abraham was visited by three angels or God himself or who? (For more information see page 37.) The Trinity has always been a difficult concept to represent pictorially, so Rublev may have chosen to represent the Trinity as three angelic visitors, all with identical faces. Traditionally, the Trinity here is seated left to right: Father, Son and Spirit.

Many scholars consider Rublev's *Trinity* to be the most perfect of all Russian icons and perhaps the most perfect of all icons ever painted.

 What, if anything, does this icon add to your understanding of angelic encounters?

El Greco, who began life in Crete but moved between Spain, Rome and Venice, painted several pictures of the Annunciation between 1568 and 1596. Most are now found in Museo Del Prado in Madrid. Look at the background of one of these, focusing particularly on the use of light and colour, the sense of movement, of balance of the real and the ethereal, the cherubs and facial expressions.

 What, if anything, do these images add to your understanding of how Gabriel brought his message to Mary?

Taking it further

Paul's letter to the Colossians is concerned principally with exalting Jesus above all others. Part of his concern was to correct some of the wrong practices and perspectives of this young church. In chapter two Paul warns them against basing their lives on anything other than Christ himself. Some were clearly interested in New Age-style philosophies or lifestyles; some were keen on 'super-spiritual' practices involving special diets and rituals (Colossians 2:16). It may be that they were even worshipping angels (verse 18).

Perhaps that would not be surprising, given that angels reflect the glory of God and in the Bible people are cautioned against worshipping them several times. However, it is more likely that these young Christians in Colossae imagined they were involved in some kind of worship *alongside* angels – joining in with what angels were doing in some visionary or ecstatic way. Remember that in 1 Corinthians 13:1 Paul says some believed they may even be inspired to speak in the tongues of angels.

Anyway, Paul makes it clear anything resembling worship towards angels is out of order for Christians who are called to be devoted to Jesus and no one and nothing else (verses 18,19). A good closing thought in a book committed to learning more about angels! More than anything, our wish as authors is that this material has led you to worship God in a fresh way. That is what the angels themselves most desire!

Review cards

Give everyone a blank postcard which they address to themselves. Invite them to draw an angelic image or symbol on the other side, or write a note to themselves, mentioning the key discoveries they have made during ANGELS. People can take their cards away to pin up somewhere they'll notice it occasionally; or use as a bookmark; or you could appoint someone to post all the cards out to everyone in a month's time, as a reminder of all they learned and experienced together.

Real experiences

RESCUE IN NICARAGUA

We were in Managua, Nicaragua, in 1998 in the aftermath of Hurricane Mitch which had caused devastating flooding across much of Central America. Managua is a very rundown capital with no heart – destroyed by an earthquake in the 1970s.

We decided to walk to the edge of Lake Nicaragua to see the extent of the flooding for ourselves. We were conspicuous, being foreign backpackers and some way off the beaten track, in a very poor area of the city. We were used to such circumstances but all of a sudden we began to feel extremely uneasy and aware of what easy targets we were.

As we struggled to re-orientate ourselves and make our way back to the main streets, a man approached us. He ran his finger across his throat indicating that we were in serious danger. He beckoned us to follow him. Not knowing whether to trust him or not, we felt we had no choice. As he led us away, he spoke to people who were hanging about. He seemed to have the authority to make them leave us alone. Eventually we found ourselves on one of the main dual carriageways leading into the centre of Managua.

Neither of us have any recollection of when the man left us. We never said goodbye to him. But we certainly felt very certain that God had been involved in keeping us safe.

UNSEEN COMPANIONS

I was doing my teaching practice in a school on the edge of town and had to walk along a lonely road to get to the school. To walk back along the road was a pretty miserable, dark and scary end to each day.

One Sunday morning, someone from church said they had driven past me one evening that week and was about to offer me a lift – but as I had two companions with me, they drove by!

I asked if they were sure it was me!

'Oh, yes,' they replied.

If these weren't angelic companions, I don't know who they were!

Drama script: Gabriel's visits to Zechariah and Mary

(from *The Dramatised Bible*)

Narrator 1:   During the time when Herod was king of Judea, there was a priest named Zechariah, who belonged to the priestly order of Abijah. His wife's name was Elizabeth; she also belonged to a priestly family.

Narrator 2:   They both lived good lives in God's sight and obeyed fully all the Lord's laws and commands. They had no children because Elizabeth could not have any, and she and Zechariah were both very old.

Narrator 1:   One day Zechariah was doing his work as a priest in the Temple, taking his turn in the daily service.

Narrator 2:   According to the custom followed by the priests, he was chosen by lot to burn incense on the altar.

Narrator 1:   So he went to the Temple of the Lord, while the crowd of people outside prayed during the hour when the incense was burnt. An angel of the Lord appeared to him, standing on the right of the altar where the incense was burnt. When Zechariah saw him, he was alarmed and felt afraid.

Gabriel: Don't be afraid, Zechariah! God has heard your prayer, and your wife Elizabeth will bear you a son. You are to name him John. How glad and happy you will be, and how happy many others will be when he is born! He will be a great man in the Lord's sight … He will go ahead of the Lord, strong and mighty like the prophet Elijah …

Zechariah: How shall I know if this is so? I am an old man, and my wife is old also.

Gabriel: I am Gabriel. I stand in the presence of God, who sent me to speak to you and tell you this good news. But you have not believed my message, which will come true at the right time. Because you have not believed, you will be unable to speak; you will remain silent until the day my promise to you comes true.

(Pause.)

Narrator 2:   In the sixth month, God sent the angel Gabriel to Nazareth … to a virgin pledged to be married to a man named Joseph, a descendant of David. The virgin's name was Mary.

Gabriel: Greetings, you who are highly favoured! The Lord is with you.

Narrator 1:   Mary was greatly troubled at his words and wondered what kind of greeting this might be.

Gabriel: Do not be afraid, Mary, you have found favour with God. You will be with child and give birth to a son, and you are to give him the name Jesus. He will be great and will be called the Son of the Most High. The Lord God will give him the throne of his father David, and he will reign over the house of Jacob for ever; his kingdom will never end.

Mary: How will this be, since I am a virgin?

Gabriel: The Holy Spirit will come upon you, and the power of the Most High will overshadow you. So the holy one to be born will be called the Son of God.

Mary: I am the Lord's servant. May it be to me as you have said.

Drama script: The angels' visit to the shepherds

(from *The Dramatised Bible*)

Narrator: There were shepherds living out in the fields near Bethlehem, keeping watch over their flocks at night. An angel of the Lord appeared to them, and the glory of the Lord shone around them, and they were terrified.

Angel: Do not be afraid. I bring you good news of great joy that will be for all the people. Today in the town of David a Saviour has been born to you; he is Christ the Lord. This will be a sign to you: You will find a baby wrapped in cloths and lying in a manger.

Narrator: Suddenly a great company of the heavenly host appeared with the angel, praising God.

Angels (all): Glory to God in the highest
And on earth peace to all on whom his favour rests.

Narrator: When the angels had left them and gone into heaven, the shepherds said to one another:

Shepherd 1: Let's go to Bethlehem—

Shepherd 2: And see this thing that has happened—

Shepherd 3: Which the Lord has told us about.

Narrator: So they hurried off and found Mary and Joseph, and the baby, who was lying in the manger. When they had seen him, they spread the word concerning what had been told them about this child, and all who heard it were amazed at what the shepherds said to them. But Mary treasured up all these things and pondered them in her heart. The shepherds returned, glorifying and praising God for all the things they had heard and seen, which were just as they had been told.

Heavenly visitation

March 24th 4 BC (Earth Time)

I have just sent Gabriel off on his second visit to Earth since this campaign began. (The first was to an elderly priest in the Temple at Jerusalem.) I expended considerable effort trying to calm him down before he left. At his last appearance he rendered the man speechless with fear. Today's visit is to a mere teenager and Gabriel is so excited I am concerned that he will terrify the poor girl.

'Oh, Oriel,' he said, dismissively, 'Humans are much more robust when they're young.'

We did agree that our Boss was unlikely to choose a girl who would be scared witless at the sight of an Angel but I still urged him to be careful.

'These humans are fragile,' I reminded him, 'You only have to appear a fraction too strongly and their faint bodies simply burn up.'

'Oriel, why do you think the Boss gave this responsibility to me?'

The truth of his reply stung me like medicine on an open wound.

'You get on with the administration,' he suggested, 'And leave the humans to me.'

Gabriel realised how sharply his words had struck their target and paused.

'I know that you are better with humans than the rest of us,' I conceded, 'But they barely know that there is more than one Archangel. And here I am, arranging rotas for millions of other Angels whose hard work will never be acknowledged, let alone remembered.'

Gabriel spotted this – my notebook – and said, 'Are you going to write the whole thing up? What an excellent idea! You had better check it out with Michael though, in case you breach his security measures.'

To be honest, the idea of an official record had not crossed my mind. From my vantage point outside of time, it is difficult to place events in what humans would understand as 'historical order' but it is possible.

'I could do,' I replied.

'You should do.'

'I will call Michael.'

Gabriel smiled, 'I'll be off. I have a lady to frighten.'

I swallowed his bait. 'Gabriel!' I yelled.

An extract from *Oriel's Diary* © Robert Harrison published by Scripture Union and used with permission.

Personal Journey

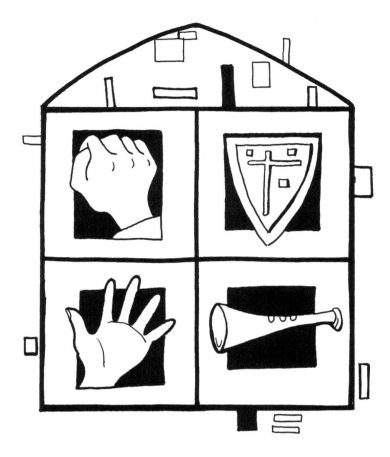

The readings and questions in this **Personal Journey** section are provided to help you explore the subject of angels throughout the Bible, particularly if you are studying alone. The readings are split into four parts, each a development of the theme in the four sessions in the first part of the book. We encourage you to use this section as your own journal, recording your thoughts, impressions and questions as you work through the Bible verses.

This is not an exhaustive set of readings. For example, several people after the trial wanted to include something on Balaam's donkey who encountered an angel barring the way. Others wanted something about the angel who guarded the entrance to the Garden of Eden. We could not include everything. But there is nothing to stop you using a Bible reference book to extend your personal study of angels. Feel encouraged to do so!

If you are only using this book as part of a group, the readings can extend the group discussion. Since this book is a photocopiable resource, you can also give out copies to the group to take home if they want to do further study between meetings.

1

ANGELS OF POWER
– GOD'S TASKFORCE

As you reflect on these readings, ask God to increase your expectation of experiencing God's power in your life.

Daniel 6:1–24

In the lions' pit, Daniel was in a similar danger to Peter in Acts 12, but perhaps far more immediately petrifying! Look at how Daniel did not praise the angel but focused on the one who had sent this angel. In fact, the angel's intervention is almost played down; certainly it's not dwelt on at any length. This is rather surprising for a book which has more to say about heaven and angels than most.

In chapter 7 Daniel describes the heavenly court where God holds sway, complete with those unnamed multitudes who stand serving before his throne (Daniel 7:9,10). In 9:20–27 the angel Gabriel appears to Daniel and in chapters 10 and 11 Daniel receives messages from a terrifying angelic visitor.

 What does all this say about angels – and God?

Matthew 2:13–15

Joseph was not aware of the danger he was in until the angel's message in a dream. Of course, dreams are just one avenue angels tread to convey their message. God's protection and power might be experienced in many ways. Sometimes escape might be the wise and godly thing to do. Joseph needed to take action himself.

 How might God warn *you* of danger?

Matthew 4:1-11; Psalm 91

The devil can quote scripture to cunning effect. In our readings from Daniel and the story about Joseph, we see that the temptation to presume upon God is always there. Of course, angels *could* rescue a man falling from the top of the temple. They surround us, ready to act at God's every command. The devil puts that suggestion to Jesus. However, the undoubted presence and power of God's angels must not be taken as evidence that it will always be God's intention to release them into action.

 What is the Psalmist saying about the power of angels? How does the devil abuse that expectation of angels? Notice Jesus' experience of angels at the end of his time of testing.

Revelation 12:7–12

This is the one clear reference to God's angels at war with those belonging to the evil one. Picture the great battle which is described here. Christians live in a world of danger and evil.

 What confidence does this message give you?

Luke 22:39–46

Jesus was in danger and he knew it. His fear almost overwhelmed him. At such a time, angelic support would seem to be just what was needed. We have seen how powerful and strong they are. As he pleaded with his father, an angel came to comfort him.

 What sort of comfort might it have been? Remember, 'comfort' literally means 'with strength/power'.

At the end of these readings, use the space here to make a note of what you have understood about angels so far, or what questions have been raised for you.

2

ANGELS OF PROTECTION
– GOD'S UNSEEN PROTECTORS

Hebrews 13:2

The last chapter of Hebrews is full of practical advice. It may be that the writer has in mind Genesis 18:1–15, where Abraham and Sarah offered hospitality to some unexpected heavenly visitors. It appears that, as with the protection God offers through his angels, it is possible that angels have performed many functions to our benefit which we are unaware of.

 What motivates you to offer hospitality to others?

 How might our 'stranger danger' society conflict with this instruction to entertain strangers?

 What insight does this verse offer into how angels operate?

Genesis 32:22–31

Jacob was about to meet his long-estranged brother Esau as he ran away from his father-in-law. His fear was genuine and deep. Throughout this one long night, he wrestled with an unknown man – an angel or God himself. This angel was not exactly protecting him.

What is your understanding of what was going on between God and Jacob here? **The artist's view** on page 24 may help you.

In scripture, angels are sometimes mediating the very presence of God to people. This was not the first time Jacob had experienced God's angels. In Genesis 28:10–22 Jacob dreamt of a ladder of angels leading up to the very presence of God. In John 1:43–51, Jesus reflects this story, stating that *he* is now the way up to God. In his fight with Jacob, however, God was certainly teaching Jacob a lesson he was never able to forget. It was at this point that Jacob acquires a new name: 'Israel' (32:28). It is as though the people of Israel were born at the point of their ancestor's struggle with God and his lameness. They needed to remember that (verse 32)!

Joshua 5:13–15

As leader of the people of Israel, Joshua was preparing for the battle over the city of Jericho. This was a key moment in Israel's conquest of the Promised Land.

 What is there to say about the man he met on his walk to spy out the lie of the land?

 Why do you think the man said he was on holy ground?

 Where does the distinction lie between an angel and the Lord?

It is unclear whether Joshua encountered God himself, an angel or a 'man'. Many Christians have taken this 'man' to be Christ in a pre-existent form. The 'man's' reply to Joshua's challenge to take sides is fascinating: 'Neither'. All armies like to think that in some way their god will be on their side. But it is not as simple as that. Even though angels may be sent to serve God's people (see Hebrews 1:14) they remain firmly under God's command, not ours. They do not take sides in the conventional way and, like God himself, they must not be presumed upon.

Matthew 18:6–11

 What does Jesus appear to be implying about the task of angels in preventing children (and adults) from sin or harm in any way?

Many Christians believe in 'guardian angels'. Certainly Jesus may be understood to be endorsing this idea in Matthew 18. And it may be a very comforting idea. But is there really any evidence for children (or anyone else for that matter) having a particular angel assigned to them? Some other scriptures encourage such a thought (see, for example, Daniel 10:13,20; 12:1). Yet, Calvin concludes, '… the care of each one of us is not the task of one angel only, but all with one consent watch over our salvation.'

 What do *you* think about guardian angels? Are they really there? What do they do? Can we communicate with them? Does each person have their very own named guardian angel?

Ephesians 6:10–20

We ought to be fully aware of the spiritual battle around us. Paul was writing to Christians who firmly believed in the spiritual realm. Look at the way he describes the battle.

Make a list of all the resources available to us to be victorious.

 Why do you think angels do not get a mention here? Need it leave them redundant?

Look back over all you have discovered about angels in these readings and note down anything you particularly want to remember.

3
ANGELS OF PRAISE
– GOD'S WORSHIPPERS

As you come to these readings, spend a few minutes worshipping God the Father, Son and Spirit for all that he is and all he has done. Remind yourself that you are joining in with the whole of redeemed creation!

Isaiah 6:1–8

This is Isaiah's account of his own call and commissioning. There are others in scripture, which you may also want to look at:

— Genesis 12:1–9 (Abraham)
— Exodus 3:1–6 (Moses)
— Jeremiah 1
— Ezekiel 1
— Acts 9 (Paul)

It is interesting to note the different ways in which God approaches the individuals involved. Isaiah was called in a spectacular way to minister to God's people at a very difficult time following the death of King Uzziah. His vision is full of colour, movement and noise. Notice Isaiah's response. He does not join in; he cannot.

 How might the worship of all creation make us aware of our own sinfulness?

 How does this vision of God's majesty and his angelic host in Isaiah 6 affect your view of the everyday world of petty intrigue, meanness, anxiety and helplessness?

Luke 2:8–16

This very familiar story is almost always looked at from the point of the shepherds or of the baby and his parents. As you read this, try to see the story from the angels' perspective (compare *Oriel's Diary!*).

 Did the rest of creation join in with them?

Philippians 2:6–11

This passage links in with Revelation 4 and 5 in that it envisages heaven as the place where all of creation will offer praise to God. Jesus' name is above all names, including angels (those in heaven). They will willingly worship him and cry out, 'Jesus is Lord'. But many others will also be doing that. Of course, Paul recognises that this worship comes as a result of Jesus' astounding humility and servanthood – to the point of the cross. Paul sees this as behaviour to be copied by humanity. Worship always has an ethical dimension in that it is tightly bound up with our day-to-day lives. Angels, of course, spend their lives in the service of God and his people. And worship is a logical part of that.

Offer your own words of praise to the Son, along with the rest of creation. Write them down, if you wish.

Hebrews 1

This is a key passage in understanding how the early church had come to understand angels. Don't forget to meditate on the glorious description of Jesus in Hebrews 1:1–4. Angels are inferior to Jesus and existed before him, says the writer.

 What else do you learn about angels from these verses? Make a note of all the ways in which angels fall short of God's Son, while still being God's servants and doing his bidding on our behalf.

Revelation 7

This vision is awe-inspiring. The saints who have already died now stand before the throne of God. Verses 1–8 seem to refer simply to the Old Testament people of Israel. But from verse 9 the field is wide open and worship is offered from all peoples and nations. The 144,000 indicate the completeness of the people of God – the full number of God's faithful people. The angels fall face down (verse 11).

If you can, kneel down and slowly read verses 9–17, allowing their power and beauty to fill you.

 What new discoveries have you made about angels from these Bible verses?

4

ANGELS OF PROCLAMATION
– GOD'S MESSENGERS

As you come to read about angels as messengers of God, pray for God's help in listening to him – ask that you will be able to discern if he is giving you a message, whether or not it is via an angel.

Genesis 18:1–15

If possible, look at Rublev's famous icon alongside the Bible passages. Abraham's visitors may have been the Trinity. This is the view of the Orthodox tradition. Or it could be three angels. It is actually quite unclear as to who these visitors are. Hebrews 13:2 may be referring to this incident, in which case they must be angels. There are similarities between this incident and the message which Gabriel has to deliver to both Zechariah and Mary. Both concern the birth of a very significant baby.

 If they were angels, what does this say about angelic appearances? At what point do you think Abraham discerned that these were no ordinary visitors?

Galatians 3:19,20; Exodus 19 and 20

The two verses in Galatians are a comment on the giving of the Law in Exodus 19 and 20. After reading Galatians, turn to the chapters in Exodus.

 What does Paul's statement in Galatians suggest about the role of angels as message-givers?

Paul does not over-estimate the ministry of the angels. His point in Galatians is that the Law was not given directly by God but mediated by angels. He wants to exalt the ministry of Jesus.

 Is it possible to over-estimate the significance of angels?

Paul is not dazzled. It certainly seems that some people in contemporary society then and now take an excessive interest in them; instead of a respect for them, they experience something which borders on or may even become an unhealthy and obsessive fascination. It's worth remembering that, in the light of this book!

Daniel 8:15–19

Daniel's vision is hard to understand. God does not deal out gratuitous mysteries, but that is not to suggest that there are no mysteries at all. There are a lot of things we cannot properly understand. However, God's purpose for his people seems to be that they should have insight into his work. Look at the parable of the sower in Mark 4:1–20. Jesus expects that many people will reject and fail to comprehend his message but his followers are to understand (Mark 4:11). In the same way, Gabriel does not satisfy everything that Daniel might have wanted to know, but he does tell him enough. We need to be satisfied with that.

 What seems to be the role of Gabriel here?

Luke 24:1–8

No exploration of angels would be complete without looking at the role of angels at the time of the resurrection. If you compare all four Gospel accounts this aspect is really quite confusing – perhaps only to be expected given the fact that the human reporters were themselves struggling to understand what happened! These verses in Luke capture the women's response to the message of the angel/two-men-in-white. If you have time, read the other resurrection accounts.

 How does the appearance of the two men help the women?

Acts 10:1–24

Once again this is a most significant event in the life of the early Church, as Peter came to realise that the good news was for non-Jews as well as Jews. Look at how the angel spoke to Cornelius, what Peter saw and heard in his vision and the role of the Holy Spirit in verse 19.

 Who was delivering what message? What might that say about the connections between angels, the Lord and the Holy Spirit?

If you have not already done so, read the Christmas story again looking out for the various times that angels proclaim God's message.

Look back at your journaling to review what has been discovered so far. You might want to follow the review card suggestion on page 41.

Use the space here to make a note of what you have understood about angels at the end of these readings.

Angels carol service

 The Christmas carol service is one event in the year when you can be sure of visitors, some of whom will not be Christians. Many churches see it as one of the major evangelistic opportunities in the year. Since angels have an appeal to people who are aware of 'spiritual' things, using angels as the theme of a carol service is an obvious avenue to explore.

The following sermon outline, based on ideas from **Lisa Holmes**, associate minister of Skipton Baptist Church, will direct your thinking.

Introduction

Identify evidence that our society is becoming more secular, yet has a deep fascination with the 'spiritual': the popularity of alternative healing; the concept of the spiritual affecting the physical; the assortment of 'mind, body, spirit' events; TV and radio programmes covering everything from the paranormal to the power of prayer; the popularity of the fantasy world of *Lord of the Rings* and *Narnia*.

How much more 'spiritual' can you get than the real story of Christmas?

— God turns over the expectations of the rich and powerful – Jesus is born in poverty and obscurity.

— The baby is both fully God and fully human – the mystery of the Incarnation; God becomes flesh!

— The mother of this precious baby is a virgin who has conceived through the power of the Holy Spirit.

— The baby lying in a cattle trough is visited and worshipped by a bunch of shepherds.

— The eastern astrologers recognise the signs of the skies and follow the star all the way to worship the newborn King in Bethlehem.

— Throughout the whole of the story we have a liberal scattering of angels!

Main message: The starring role of angels

Angels have a God-given starring role in the drama of the incarnation.

Angels – God-sent

God despatched his archangel Gabriel (he seems to get the best jobs!) to speak to Zechariah about Elizabeth's pregnancy; then on a second assignment to let Mary know that she was going to have a baby; he probably also appeared to Joseph in a dream to tell him not to worry that the baby wasn't his because it would all be OK. Then all the angels get in on the act – singing to the shepherds on the hills at Jesus' birth.

Angels – Awe-inspiring

Angels are not the chubby cherubs on your Christmas cards. When angels appear, people are filled with awe and even fear. Something of the glory and authority of God himself is invested in them. If God gives the angels scripts, the first line of each dialogue would seem to be: *Fear not!*

Angels – God-mediating

Angels are good and mediate something of the presence of God. In Luke 1:19 the angel says, 'I stand in the presence of God and I've been sent to tell you good news'. When they speak, people are reassured and listen to what is being said.

Angels – Drama-directing

Angels are the producers of the original nativity play; assigning roles as God directs them! The message of the angels is that God uses *ordinary people* to be caught up in an *extraordinary story* of hope and life where the spiritual and material worlds coincide. Maybe you never had a part in a nativity play – but you can be part of the ongoing story of God in his world.

Angels – Jesus-focused

The original story – and the ongoing story – all revolve around a central character. His name is Jesus. Robbie Williams may have sung *I'm Loving Angels Instead* but that's not what the angels want. The main role of the angels is never to draw attention to themselves but to Jesus. Zechariah and Elizabeth's baby John will prepare the way for the Lord. The angel focuses Mary on the wonder of her son (Luke 1:32,35). The same is true as the angel speaks to Joseph (Matthew 1:21–23) and the choir of angels give the same message to the shepherds (Luke 2:10,11,14).

At Christmas – with all its trappings – let's make sure we allow everything, along with the angels, to direct us to Jesus without whom it would never have happened. Jesus is the revelation of God's love and exciting purpose for our world.

Features to add in to your service:

— Christmas carols which contain references to angels – there are many to choose from.
— Bible readings which include accounts of angelic activity.
— An 'interview' with an angel.
— A dramatic presentation of the Christmas story which includes an angelic presence.
— A powerpoint presentation showing angel images.
— A reading from *Oriel's Diary*.

Angels for all ages
– an event for the whole family

This could be:

— at any time of the day or week, taking a flexible amount of time

— preparatory for Christmas or Easter

— inclusive of food – simple refreshments or a whole meal

— including games

— for those on the fringe of the church

— for all ages within the church

— follow-up to a holiday club

— a celebration for groups/ individuals who have used ANGELS – plus their guests

Decide the purpose of the event, the target audience and the best time of year. Provide a variety of options which develop the angel theme, and offer people a choice of activities. For example:

Crafts

Christmas Wrapped Up (SU) contains ideas for making blow-out angels, instant angels, angel mobiles and pop-up angel cards. These could be more or less sophisticated, depending upon the age of participants. You could make long trumpets or wings to be used by angels (but don't make them look too much like fairy wings!). Or you could use quick-dry clay and create a range of angels. If you were doing this before Easter, you would want to introduce more Spring-like options, such as an Easter garden, or bowls of bulbs which have an angelic background or decoration.

Drama

Many dramas include conversation with an angel or two. People of all ages can prepare a drama either to perform to those present or at a later service.

Angel banners

Creating angel banners to hang in church lends itself to a group activity. Alternatively, a group could create a large angel to hang up in the church using fabric, card, glitter etc. See the example from Skipton Baptist Church on page 39.

Angel voices

People of all ages can make music as a heavenly choir or band! This can be for performance to those present or at a later event.

Angel food

Either make this as part of the food to be eaten at the event (see pages 22 and 23 for suggestions) or to be taken home. Other examples: iced biscuits, gingerbread angels, angel cake, mini-pizzas cut into angel shapes.

Team and individual games

Devise these round the angels theme – for example: pin the wing on the angel, hide the angel (hunt the thimble) or message-passing games. Divide into teams named after the archangels.

You may want to show a film that features angels and there are many to choose from. But make sure that you encourage discussion which helps people distinguish between fantastical ideas which encourage stereotypical views of angels and facts from the Bible.

Suggestions for a sermon series on angels

During the time we were writing this book, we were told several times that people had never heard a sermon about angels! This is both surprising and, perhaps, to be expected! *Surprising* because angels are clearly so prominent in the Bible. *To be expected* since Protestants, in particular, have been so cautious about the rather fanciful portrayal of angels and other heavenly beings throughout Church history. They have wanted to avoid any of that sort of fantasy, preferring rightly to focus upon the Lord Jesus. However, as we have seen, angels are a significant reality in God's world and to say nothing about them in our preaching is clearly bad.

What we have been looking at in this book lends itself to exploration in a series of four sermons, looking at angels as mediators of God's power, protection, praise and proclamation.

1 Angels of power – God's taskforce

The first sermon could explore something of the nature of power as exercised by our superiors in the world today. For the most part, the Church is much less powerful and, in some countries, this is a real issue for the Church as it is persecuted and pushed around. This was very much the experience of the early Church and there are many examples of this to be found in the early chapters of Acts. Both religious and secular authorities try to bully the Church, resulting in Peter's imprisonment.

Looking especially at Acts 12:1–19, Herod's use of power could be explored: his suppression of leaders, terror tactics and threats. Peter's behaviour is worth examining: his clear confidence in God as he sleeps between the guards, and his decisiveness when the time comes to move. Most of all a sermon could explore the exercise of angelic power. God chooses to exercise his power by way of an angel. The Church cannot presume upon this, but it demonstrates God's ability to deliver his servants. Interestingly, Peter seems surprised to realise that it is an angel which has rescued him, provoking the thought that God may well have exercised his power through angels on several occasions in our own lives without our even suspecting it!

2 Angels of protection – God's secret agents

This last point is equally true when we consider our second sermon concerning the protective care afforded by angels. The biblical passage is 2 Kings 6:8–23. In our own lives we tend to take God's care and protection for granted. When we walk out of the house in the morning, what is to stop us being assaulted or being overwhelmed by something dreadful? Of course, in some parts of the world this is more likely than in others. Moreover, it is God's sustaining power which prevents the universe from imploding or disintegrating at any moment. In the biblical passage we find a specific case of God's protection through the angelic hosts. Indeed, Psalm 91 encourages readers to put their faith in God and trust his angelic powers to sustain them in the hour of need. Satan tested Jesus in the wilderness (Matthew 4) to presume upon this action of God.

Certainly God offers protection, but we can't take it for granted. In 2 Kings 6 the problem is not presumption but a failure to be aware of God's angelic presence and to have faith in God's ability to side with his people.

There is much here to encourage us to lean on God's protective power at times of crisis, whether the opposition powers are the armies of an enemy or the 'principalities and powers' spoken of by Paul in Ephesians 6:10–20. Christians have good reason to put their faith in God.

3 Angels of praise – God's worshippers

Our third sermon will focus upon the role of angels as part of God's manifold creation in praising him for his greatness and goodness. On his way into Jerusalem, Jesus spoke, ironically, of even the stones crying out in worship if humanity failed to acclaim him (Luke 19:40). The fact is that all of creation is intended to sing out in worship to God. As members of the non-fallen part of God's world, angels naturally fulfil that function. Revelation chapters 4 and 5 depict all parts of the creation worshipping – chapter 4 representing creation under the old covenant and chapter 5 under the new covenant. It is as though the angelic host are fulfilling their role just as they did at the birth of Jesus (Luke 2:14). This would be a good point at which to explore the idea of the new creation released from its suffering and groaning to glorify God in all his wonder (Romans 8:18–25).

4 Angels of proclamation – God's messengers

The fourth and final sermon could revisit that same moment, when God's Son was born to Mary. In Luke 1:26–38 we encounter the angel Gabriel delivering his wonderful message from God. The role of both angels and God's people is to bring a message of salvation and hope to this needy world. Once again humanity is potentially caught up with God's purposes for the world. Both angels and we ourselves are his servants involved in proclamation and sharing what we know of God to those around us. This final sermon could focus upon how humanity is part of a greater movement to articulate God's words alongside the rest of creation.

More angel resources published by Scripture Union

The Oriel trilogy by Robert Harrison

Oriel's Diary

A fresh take on the most significant person who ever lived! The personal diary of Archangel Oriel, colleague of Gabriel and Michael, records the birth, life, death and resurrection of Jesus Christ. Closely based on Luke's Gospel, *Oriel's Diary* presents an entirely original view of a familiar story.

Oriel's Travels

From fanatical destroyer of the followers of Jesus to fearless gospel pioneer – the incredible story of the man central to the formation of the Church! Political wranglings at the highest level … personal animosities at the lowest … the mystery of how the Church – 'the Boss's new family' – was birthed in the midst of fierce earthly discords and intense spiritual battles is described though the travel diary of Archangel Oriel.

Oriel in the Desert

What does it take to transform an unbelieving melancholic murderer into the godly leader of a new nation? The personal diary of Archangel Oriel gives us an inside track on Moses, who rises from a dysfunctional family background to engage in the intrigue of Egyptian politics. After head-to-head confrontation with his step-cousin Pharaoh Rameses II, Moses leads the escape from forced labour of the demoralised slaves who are destined to become God's chosen people.

Angels

Eight studies in the bestselling *LifeBuilder* series for individuals or groups by Douglas Connelly

In the unseen realms of the universe, powerful and wonderful beings move at the speed of light to carry out their Master's will. They are involved in the complex political affairs of the nations and in the smallest concerns of children. They guard, protect, watch over – and engage in cosmic battles of which we are completely unaware. Yet angels are the subject of much misinformation. This fascinating study guide helps us discover the truth as revealed by the Bible.

Christmas Wrapped Up

At last – the ultimate Christmas resource book! It really does contain practically everything a church might need for Christmastime. Packed full of top-quality material combining years of experience with exciting new ideas, it will help churches get the most out of Christmas.

Contains: all-age Advent service, yuletide evangelism, quotes and anecdotes, plays, quiz questions, songs, rhymes and raps, nativity services, quick Christmas talks, short presentations, Christmas day services, craft ideas, Christingle services, assembly outlines, Christmas parties and games.

Scripture Union produces a wide range of Bible reading notes for people of all ages and Bible-based material for small groups. SU publications are available from Christian bookshops. For information and to request free samples and a free catalogue of Bible resources:

— phone SU's mail order line: local rate number 08450 706006

— email info@scriptureunion.org.uk

— fax 01908 856020

— log on to www.scriptureunion.org.uk

— write to SU Mail Order, PO Box 5148, Milton Keynes MLO, MK2 2YX